THE CHERRIES: 1890 to the Premier League

DAILY ECHO

In association with:
cmp
Print Solutions

Contents:

RECORD BREAKER MAC ON THE BALL

TED MacDOUGALL holds the ball with which he set up a new FA Cup scoring record when he

FAN-TASTIC!

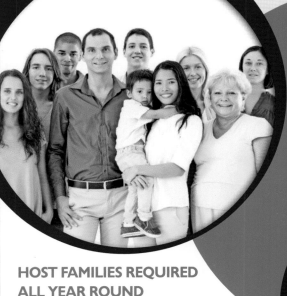

BOSCOMBE V. PORTSMOUTH. 25.12.14. 100.

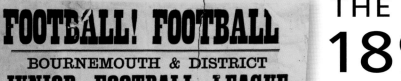

THE EARLY YEARS
1890-1949

In association with:

cmp
Print Solutions

AFC Bournemouth began life as Boscombe St John's Lads Institute FC in 1890.

But the Cherries story really began on October 7, 1899, when Boscombe FC played its first match. The venue was a pitch in Castlemain Road, the opponents were Christchurch Royal Artillery, and the visitors won 2-1.

Kings Park became the Cherries' home in 1902, and in 1910, landowner JE Cooper-Dean granted a long lease on a piece of waste ground there. Club secretary Wilf Hayward enlisted volunteers to build a stand for 300 spectators.

The club lifted the Hampshire Junior Cup in 1905-06 and made their FA Cup debut in 1913-14 but were struggling in the South-Eastern League when war cut the season short.

After the war, the club won at least one trophy a season until 1923, when they became Bournemouth and Boscombe Athletic FC and entered the Football League.

The remaining inter-war years were a period of highs and lows. The lows included twice dropping out of the League; their worst-ever season in 1933-34, with 100 goals conceded; and the first time the Cherries had to get out the begging bowl.

The highs included reaching the third round of the FA Cup in 1926-27, with 13,409 watching them at home against Liverpool; gaining a new stand for 3,700 spectators; and beating Northampton 10-0 at Dean Court, only for the outbreak of World War II the next

day to wipe the result from the record books.

In 1946, the Cherries won their first major trophy, the League Three (South) Cup, after a 136-minute semi-final replay against QPR at Shepherds Bush.

That April, a promotion battle with QPR saw 25,700 in the ground at Dean Court and 6,000 outside listening to a commentary by the secretary. It was QPR who went up that season, but a proud Boscombe set nine club records.

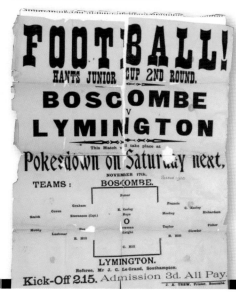

■ Boscombe FC 1899-1900 season - the first Cherries team photo (right)
■ 1908-09 (below)
■ 1910-11 (second below)

The Cherries
1899-1913

Cherries played at Castlemain Road, Pokesdown from 1899-1902 then at Kings Park from 1910

BOSCOMBE WINNERS OF WEST HANTS AND PAGE CROFT CUPS · 1912-13 PHOTO BY C 244.

Season tickets were first issued in 1912-13, grandstand tickets were 10s.6d. (ten shillings and sixpence) per year and ground season tickets were 5s

The Cherries 1913-1920

Crowd in the stands at Boscombe v Bournemouth football match, 13th April 1914

In association with:

cmp Print Solutions

BOSCOMBE V. BOURNEMOUTH JAN.3.1913 .168.

■ Spectators at Boscombe v Bournemouth 3rd January 1913(left)
■ Boscombe FC crowd 1920 (right)
■ Photo dated 28th April 1920 shows the old main stand (bottom left)
■ Boscombe FC winners Page Croft Cup 1920 (bottom right)

■ With the declaration of war, the South-Eastern League ceased to run and the club no longer played

- 1926-27 (below)
- Cartoon from The Football Echo and Sports Gazette Saturday August 8th 1926 (left)
- 1926-27 (right)
- 1931-32 (below right)
- 1932-33 (centre right)

■ The club was managed from 1923-25 by Harry Kinghorn and from 1925-28 by Leslie Knighton

The Cherries 1926-1938

In association with:
cmp
Print Solutions

■ Boscombe football team and directors annual outing 1935 (above)
■ Team 1936-37 (below)
■ Team 1937-38 (above right)
■ Boscombe team group, 1937-

38. Back row left to right: Willie Smith, Norman Millar, Len Brooks, Fred Pincott, Fred Marsden, Peter Monaghan. Front row left to right: Bob Redfern, Ernie Whittam, Harry Mardon, Willie O'Brien, Jimmy Lovery (bottom right)

■ Bob Crompton managed the team from 1935-36 and Charlie Bell from 1936-39

The Cherries
1937-1946

■ 1937 Aerial shot of Dean Court, Thistlebarrow Road (above)

In association with:

cmp
Print Solutions

■ The 1945-46
League Division 3
(South) cup winning team

Back row left to right:
Dai Woodward, Fred Rowell,
Fred Wilson, Ken Bird,
Joe Sanaghan, Paddy Gallacher

Front row: left to right:
Tommy Paton, Jack Kirkham,
Fred Marsden, Ernie Tagg,
Jack McDonald

■ Boscombe v Wolverhampton Wanderers attracts largest FA Cup tie crowd at Dean Court, January 10th 1948

■ Boscombe players Percival, Bennett and Bird training at YMCA for cup tie with Manchester United January 1949 (right)

■ Boscombe overcome a two goal half-time deficit to win their FA Cup tie 4-2 against Exeter City to inspire this cartoon in the Football Echo and Sports Gazette Saturday December 7th 1946 (below)

DEEP DEPRESSION

HA! HA! I'M FROM EXETER

Half-time:-
BOSCOMBE .. 0
EXETER CITY .. 2

I WISH I HAD NEVER LEFT THE SEA

Full-time:-
BOSCOMBE .. 4
EXETER CITY .. 2

The Cherries
1946-1948

In association with:

cmp
Print Solutions

■ Bournemouth and Boscombe Athletic team photo 1947-48 season

Boscombe gets Giant-killers' cup

The Mayor of Bournemouth (Cllr. P. G. Templeman), presenting the "Giant Killers' Cup" to Harry Hughes, Boscombe football captain, before Saturday's match at Dean Court. The cup, presented by the "Sunday Pictorial," is for the small club which puts up the best performance in the FA Cup competition. Boscombe this year defeated the Wolves and Tottenham Hotspurs — "Echo" photo.

Football broadcast for hospitals

Messrs. R. Else and A. Bush, members of Bournemouth Toc H, who made the commentary on the Boscombe v Queen's Park Rangers match on Saturday to local hospitals.—"Echo" photo.

WHO'S AFRAID OF THE BIG BAD WOLVES!

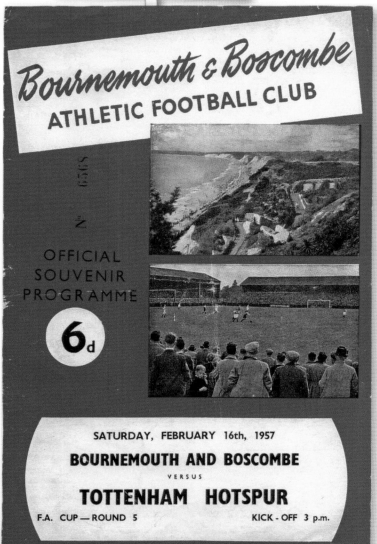

Bournemouth & Boscombe ATHLETIC FOOTBALL CLUB

N° 6565

OFFICIAL SOUVENIR PROGRAMME

6d

SATURDAY, FEBRUARY 16th, 1957

BOURNEMOUTH AND BOSCOMBE
VERSUS
TOTTENHAM HOTSPUR

F.A. CUP — ROUND 5   KICK - OFF 3 p.m.

THE FIFTIES

In association with:
cmp
Print Solutions

It was a match that would be talked about for a lifetime – the day Bournemouth and Boscombe Athletic took on the Busby Babes.

Manchester United came to Dean Court to play before a crowd of 28,799, bringing with them the astonishing crop of young players who had been nurtured by Sir Matt Busby.

Boscombe had already seen an astonishing cup run, beating Burton Albion 8-0, Swindon 1-0, Accrington Stanley 2-0, Wolves 1-0 (a result hailed as the greatest giant-killing in history) and Spurs 3-1.

Boscombe's Brian Bedford scored once, United's Johnny Berry twice. All the goals, especially United's winning penalty, were controversial, but the Cherries had made a great side sweat.

Less than a year after the match, six of that visiting team were killed in the Munich air disaster.

Cherries set a new record that year for the most goals in a season – 88 in the League, 16 in the Cup.

The match was the highlight of a decade which had started with the Cherries' golden jubilee season but had then seen some inconsistent football.

Highlights had included the signing in 1952 of Tommy Goodwin from Leicester. His recall to Eire in 1956 made him the first full international to play for Boscombe.

After the Manchester United clash, the Cherries would see a couple of mediocre seasons, finishing the decade mid-table in the new, national Division Three.

But the memory of United would last a lifetime. Busby wrote in his memoirs: "There were many great Cup occasions for United in 1956/57, yet I feel our finest hour was seen on the Dean Court ground at Bournemouth."

Cup invasion hits Wolverhampton

"ECHO" STAFF REPORTER
WOLVERHAMPTON, Saturday.

WOLVERHAMPTON WAS TODAY INVADED BY 4,000 BOSCOMBE SOCCER FANS FOR THE FOURTH ROUND F.A. CUP-TIE AT MOLINEUX.

They came in six special trains, by coach and by car.

■ John Meadows, Boscombe's goalkeeper, making a double-fisted clearance over the head of Roost, Bristol Rovers' inside-left. Boscombe won 2-0, March 1951 (left)

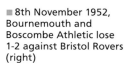

■ 8th November 1952, Bournemouth and Boscombe Athletic lose 1-2 against Bristol Rovers (right)

■ 17th September 1952, Bournemouth and Boscombe Athletic lose 2-1 against Newport County (below)

■ Tommy Godwin tries an acrobatic save while Jack Fisher watches on, 7th November 1953

**The Cherries
1950-1953**

In association with:
cmp
Print Solutions

■ Joseph "Joe" Brown played for Boscombe from 1954-59

The Cherries
1954-1955

■ 21st August 1954, Coventry City beat Bournemouth and Boscombe Athletic 1-0

■ Derek Leaver going for goal. 24th August 1955. Bournemouth and Boscombe Athletic beat Colchester United 3-1 (left)

■ Charles "Charlie" Gallogly played as a fullback for Huddersfield Town, Watford and Bournemouth (right). In 1950 he won two caps for Northern Ireland

■ 9th October 1954, Bournemouth and Boscombe Athletic beaten 1-0 by Millwall (below)

■ Bournemouth & Boscombe Athletic 1959-60 (above)

■ The new-look Brighton Beach End for Boscombe fans at Dean Court in July 1957 (right)

■ Panoramic shot of Dean Court featuring a match against Brentford in October 1959 (below)

The Cherries 1957-1960

In association with:

cmp Print Solutions

■ Bournemouth & Boscombe Athletic arriving at Bradford in 1960

led-zip

LED LIGHTING SPECIALISTS

Led-Zip Lighting is an independently run, award-winning, Bournemouth based LED lighting distributor and lighting consultant company, with unique bespoke manufacturing capabilities with a showroom located in Northbourne.

We supply and provide expert advice and high quality light fittings to both trade, and retail customers.

Call our sales team in the office today.

led-zip.co.uk | 01202 577 400 | info@led-zip.co.uk

Bournemouth & Boscombe ATHLETIC FOOTBALL CLUB

Official Programme 6d

SATURDAY, 8th JANUARY, 1966
BOURNEMOUTH AND BOSCOMBE
versus
QUEEN'S PARK RANGERS
DIVISION III KICK-OFF 3 p.m.

Match of decade grips Bournemouth

£885,000 grant for B'mouth by-pass

'AIN'T GOT THIS THOUGH,' said the gentleman with the sideboards and the red-and-white scarf

No doubt this time, and it's...
BOSCOMBE'S THREE GOAL SHOCK FOR BURY TOWN

BOURNEMOUTH & BOSCOMBE ATHLETIC FOOTBALL CLUB

OFFICIAL PROGRAMME

CUP PHOTO-SPECIAL

FOUR MINUTES TO GO...
By Colin Smith

Liverpool skipper

IT IS FOUR MINUTES FROM TIME AND BOSCOMBE, A GOAL UP IN THEIR F.A. CUP CLASH AT DEAN COURT, ARE STUNNED BY A DISPUTED LIVERPOOL EQUALISER. IT'S A DRAW, AND A REPLAY AT ANFIELD IS REQUIRED.

WEDNESDAY, 20th NOVEMBER, 1968
BOURNEMOUTH & BOSCOMBE
versus
BURY TOWN
F.A. CUP — ROUND 1 (Replay)
KICK - OFF 7.30 p.m. 1/-

THE SIXTIES

In association with:
cmp
Print Solutions

In the decade when England celebrated its national team's World Cup triumph, the action at Dean Court was often a lot less inspiring.

Starting the decade mid-table in Division Three, Boscombe struggled, and manager Don Welsh was sacked in 1961.

His replacement was the team's first player-manager, Bill McGarry, who had captained Huddersfield and been capped for England four times.

McGarry presided over a recovery, and even a shot at promotion in 1962-63. His successor, Reg Flewin, also led a serious promotion challenge.

Freddie Cox succeeded him for a second stint as manager, but the Cherries were plagued by declining gates (below 4,000 at the end of 1965), cash shortages and disappointing results. They finished 20th in the division in 1966-67.

But there were morale-boosting occasions too. In January 1968, a Dean Court crowd of 24,388 saw the Cherries apply pressure to a Liverpool team that included Emlyn Hughes, Ian Callaghan and Ian St John. The goalless FA Cup third round match led to a replay at Anfield, when Boscombe played strongly but were defeated 4-1.

The same year saw ex-player Dickie Dowsett launch the Cherry Bees fundraising initiative, plus the opening of a supporters club. Kick-offs at 7.30pm on Saturdays until the end of September were designed to draw holiday-makers and those who played other sports on Saturday afternoons.

The team were playing sufficiently well to be promotion hopefuls in 1968-69. That would all go sour the following season, but in the summer of 1969, Cox spent perhaps the best £10,000 the club had ever parted with – buying a young striker named Ted MacDougall.

■ Cllr WJ Wareham, president of Dean Court football supporters club, handing over new metal gates at Dean Court to chairman Reg Hayward, to commemorate the diamond jubilee of the club (left)

■ Boscombe Football Club chairman Mr RT Hayward, holding the Pickford Cup, and manager Don Welsh chat to ground staff boys Bob Trote, Chris Reading, Tony Adlen, Tony Byrne and Ray Massey at the Bournemouth Pavilion Feb 1960 (below)

■ Aerial view of Boscombe including AFC Bournemouth and Boscombe railway line, taken in 1960 (top right)

■ Match action from April 1961 (right)

In association with:

cmp
Print Solutions

The Cherries
1960-1962

■ Construction of Dean Court tower bases for the new floodlights in June 1961

■ Boscombe and Bournemouth Athletic team from 4th November 1961 (right)

■ Match action from 16th September 1961 (bottom right)

The Cherries 1962-1964

- Team photo for the 1962-63 season (top left)
- Denis Coughlin misses a penalty as Bournemouth draw 1-1 with Walsall in April 1964 (left)
- Action from the 1962-63 season (above)
- Team photo for the 1963-64 season (below)

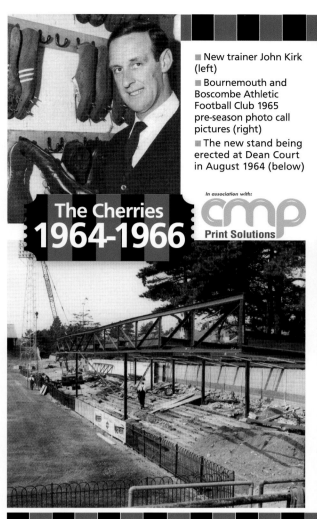

■ New trainer John Kirk (left)
■ Bournemouth and Boscombe Athletic Football Club 1965 pre-season photo call pictures (right)
■ The new stand being erected at Dean Court in August 1964 (below)

The Cherries 1964-1966

In association with:
cmp Print Solutions

THE CHERRIES: 1890 to the Premier League

■ In early 1966 Bournemouth draw Burnley in the FA Cup 3rd round...

...Bournemouth earn a 1-1 draw at home, but in the replay fans see their team beaten 7-0 at Burnley

■ New floodlights being used by Cherries fans to get a better view (left)
■ Bournemouth and Boscombe team 22nd October 1965 (above)

■ Keeper David Best in FA Cup action against Weymouth on 13th November 1965. They drew 0-0, but won the replay in Weymouth 1-4 (below)

In association with:

cmp
Print Solutions

■ Bournemouth manager Freddie Cox contemplates how his team can beat Burnley FC in the FA Cup 3rd round at Dean Court. The match ended in a 1-1 draw

■ Home fans cheer on as Boscombe draw the FA Cup match against Burnley 1-1 (above)

■ Tony Hancock in the crowd at Dean Court for the FA Cup match against Burnley (below)

■ The Bournemouth team and enthusiastic fans travel a full 24 hours by train to see the FA Cup 3rd round replay against Burnley (left and above)

■ Bournemouth lose the match 7-0, Andy Lochhead (on knees), Dave Merrington (arms raised), and goalie Dave Best (below)

The Cherries 1965-1966

In association with: **cmp Print Solutions**

The Cherries
1965-1966

In association with:
cmp
Print Solutions

■ Bournemouth and Boscombe Athletic v Oldham Athletic, 27th August 1966, Bournemouth won 2-1

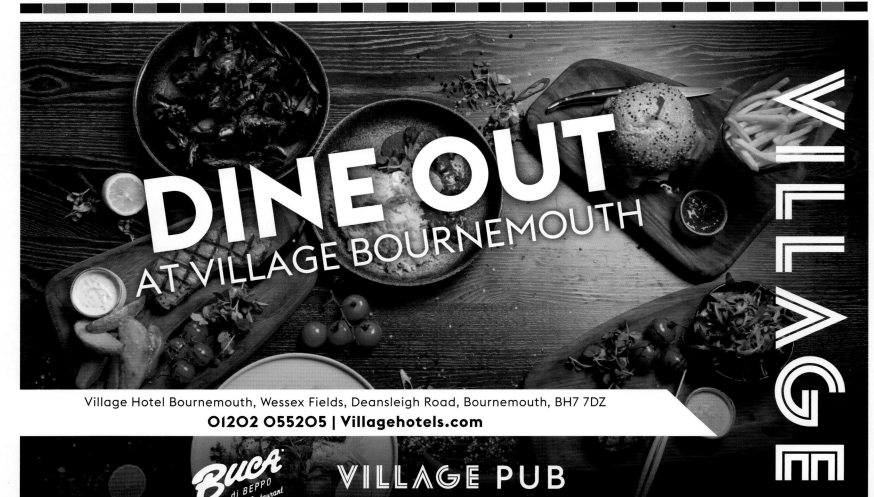

The Cherries 1966-1967

In association with:

cmp Print Solutions

■ Bournemouth and Boscombe Athletic v Torquay United, 1st October 1966. Bournemouth won 1-0.

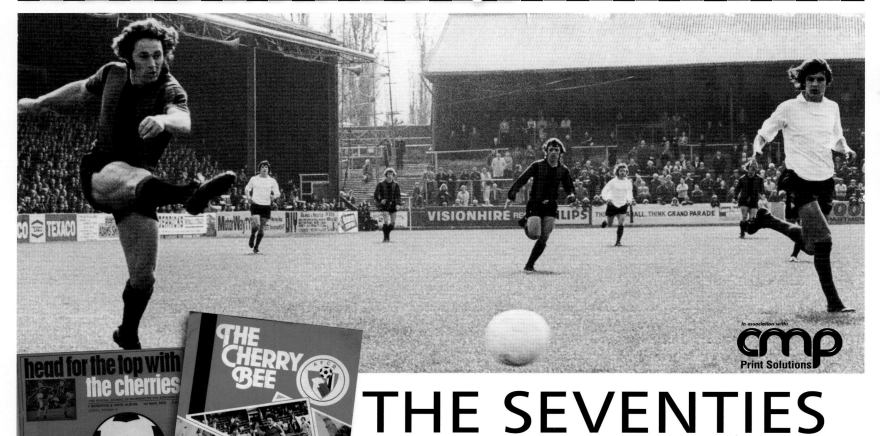

In association with:
cmp Print Solutions

THE SEVENTIES

It was the decade of Supermac.

The Cherries started the 1970s by being relegated to the Fourth Division, but bounced straight back up with the aid of one of the club's legends.

MacDougall set a club record of 49 goals in that season of 1970-71, including six against Oxford City in the FA Cup.

Manager John Bond strengthened the squad with further signings, including Phil Boyer, with whom MacDougall continued the phenomenal partnership which had begun at York.

Bond also introduced the name

AFC Bournemouth and adopted red and black shirts inspired by AC Milan.

The Cherries were on top form again for most of 1971-72, with MacDougall scoring nine goals in the 11-0 demolition of Margate in the FA Cup. But their form slipped later on and they missed out on promotion.

Bond made two more key signings: Jimmy Gabriel from Southampton and Harry Redknapp from West Ham. But in September 1972, MacDougall was bought by Manchester United for £200,000. For the second time in a

row, the Cherries narrowly missed out on promotion.

John Bond was lured to Norwich in 1973, along with coach Ken Brown, followed by a succession of key players.

One of those, John Benson, returned to Dean Court as player-manager in 1978, by which time the club was troublingly close to dropping out of the Fourth Division.

MacDougall was also back in November 1978, but too many games were going the wrong way, and Benson quit.

New manager Alec Stock presided over a morale-boosting 7-1 win against Doncaster – but few could have predicted the success that would follow in just a few years.

RECORD BREAKER MAC ON THE BALL

TED MacDOUGALL holds the ball with which he set up a new FA Cup scoring record when he hit nine of the 11 against Margate in the First Round tie at Dean Court on Saturday.

head for the top with the cherries
THE OFFICIAL JOURNAL OF A.F.C. BOURNEMOUTH

A.F.C. Bournemouth v Halifax Town F.C.
LEAGUE DIVISION III   29th August, 1972   7.30 pm

THE OFFICIAL JOURNAL OF AFC BOURNEMOUTH
season 1976/77

AFC BOURNEMOUTH
v
WORKINGTON
TUESDAY, 24th AUGUST, 1976
Football League Division Four

■ Dennis Allen in action during Bournemouth v Workington 23rd September 1970, they won 1-0, League Division 4 (left)

■ West Ham's Billy Bonds and Bournemouth's David Stocks await the fall of the coin in a pre-season practice game (right)

■ Training in the snow on the Fernheath Road ground. Led by Keith Miller, Trevor Hartley and John Sainty (below)

The Cherries
1970-1971

In association with:
cmp
Print Solutions

■ Ted MacDougal and Phil Boyer l in sombrero hats looking forward to the 1970 World Cup in Mexico (right)

■ Bournemouth team 1st May 1971 (left)

■ John Bond in talks with West Ham's Harry Redknapp in December 1970. He transferred two years later for £31,000 (right)

■ Harold Walker and Ken Brown share a joke with the team after 8-1 win at Dean Court in the FA Cup replay against Oxford City in November 1970 (bottom right)

■ Alan Sharp of the Coverdale Organisation discusses 'positive play as a result of positive thinking' training scheme with John Bond, Ken Brown, Harold Walker and Reg Tyrell (below)

■ Manager John Bond with new signing goalkeeper Fred Davies

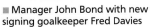

Record breaker Ted MacDougall scores nine of the eleven goals against Margate in the FA Cup first round tie November 1971

■ John Bond and 14 year old son Kevin (above)

■ An extra 1,000 seats are installed for Cherries' match against Aston Villa, October 1971 (right)

■ Cherries ace goal-scorer Ted MacDougall poses with nine footballs to represent his triple hat-trick in the FA Cup against Margate (left)

The Cherries 1971-1972

In association with:
cmp Print Solutions

■ Ted MacDougall receives his player of the month award for November from John Bond and Harold Walker in the Dean Court Supporters' Social Club (left)

■ John Sainty, John Benson, Fred Davies and Keith Miller take an 11am plunge with the Spartans (below left)

■ Harold Walker, Chairman (below)

■ A fan's unusual perch at Dean Court to watch his team draw 1-1 with Brighton (right)

■ Cherries beat Grimsby 1-0, pictured Phil Boyer (above)

■ Harry Redknapp joins Division Three Bournemouth in 1972 from West Ham United, he watches the pre-season friendly against Tottenham as injury prevents him from playing (right)

■ The squad from August 1972 (below)

■ Cherries cup squad for the FA Cup game against Newcastle United (left)

■ Newcastle United v Bournemouth. Cherries are beaten by two goals in two minutes midway through the first half (bottom left)

■ Harry Redknapp in action (bottom centre)

■ AFC Bournemouth v Oldham. Brian Clark leaps as Cherries slip into gear for the final push for promotion (right)

■ Jimmy Gabriel against Halifax in April (bottom right)

The Cherries 1972-1973

■ The club name changed to AFC Bournemouth in 1972 as manager John Bond and Chairman Harold Walker wanted to give the club a more continental feel

■ Keeper David Best returns to Cherries after a gap of nine years

■ AFC Bournemouth v Darlington. Cherries lost 1-2 (left)

■ Police clear the stands and terraces to conduct a search after a bomb scare during the second half of Cherries' game against Southport. Nothing was found and the match was resumed and finished 3-3 (below)

The Cherries 1975-1976

In association with:
cmp Print Solutions

The Cherries 1976-1977

■ Meet the new Cherries. Tom Paterson, Hughen Riley, Frank Barton and Peter Johnson, August 1976 (above)

■ AFC Bournemouth v Newport County (above right)

■ AFC Bournemouth shoot for the sun. Players have added incentive this season with the player of the year winning a holiday for two in Tenerife courtesy of John Plank Travel. A holiday in Majorca is also up for grabs for the first player to score 20 goals. John Plank is pictured donning the club strip and shooting for goal (right)

■ AFC Bournemouth venture into the 1976-77 campaign in the Fourth Division with a pool of just 16 players

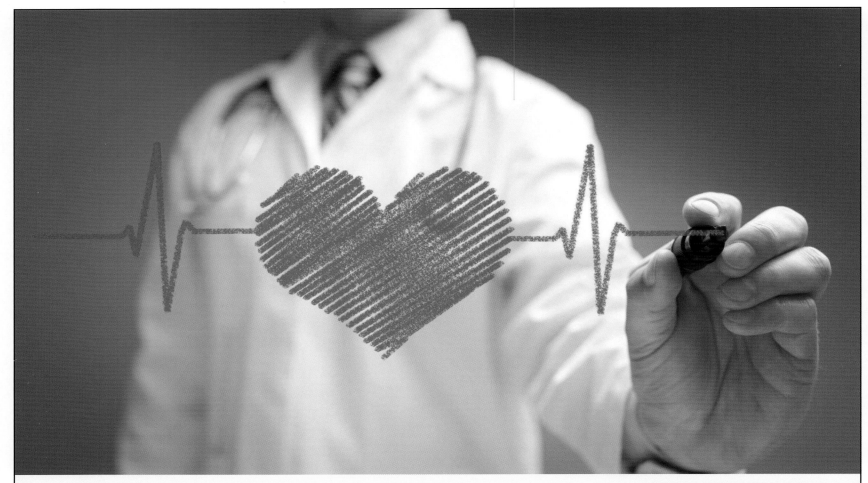

Join us in the Heart Age Challenge

Find out your heart age using the latest technology and then follow a program to lower your heart age!

Total Health Group, founded by Jeffrey Finch, has been established to test and educate the nation in *cardiovascular health*.

" *Having been a professional footballer for over 20 years I was able to train longer, lowered my heart age and recovered quicker following my test and the nutritional advise that Jeff gave me.* "

Steve Fletcher - AFC Bournemouth

jeffrey@totalhealthgroup.co.uk   07772 890348

@totalhealthgroup totalhealthgroup

www.totalhealthgroup.co.uk

THE EIGHTIES

IT is hard to believe now that Harry Redknapp's first experience of managing the Cherries saw the club lose 9-0 to Lincoln and 5-0 to Leyton Orient.

That was in the season of 1982-83, when manager Dave Webb had been sacked after a string of poor results and Redknapp was filling in on a caretaker basis.

That season, Bournemouth had been in the headlines for signing George Best. But the once-great star played only five times, and the team ended that season in 14th place.

Redknapp became permanent manager after the 1983-84 season got off to a poor start and manager Don Megson quit.

The club began 1984 with the kind of giant-killing FA Cup tie that comes once in a generation – a 2-0 defeat of Manchester United in front of 15,000 at Dean Court. Bournemouth dominated the game and Redknapp called it "the greatest day of my football life".

But there was more success to come. While that season's League performance was less impressive, they were looking like promotion candidates the following year, and in 1987 the Cherries were finally going up after topping Division Three.

The club's fortunes fluctuated wildly in their first season in Division Two, and they started the 1988-89 season as relegation favourites. Behind the scenes, a succession of take-overs and cash shortages did little to make the squad feel secure.

But, boosted by the inspired signing of prolific goal-scorer Luther Blissett from Watford, the Cherries clung on. And by the dawn of the 1990s, Redknapp was the club's longest-serving manager.

■ AFC Bournemouth team photo 1980-81 (right)

■ AFC team 1982: left to right, back row : Ian Leigh, Howard Goddard, Phil Brignull, Nigel Spackman, Tom Heffernan, Kenny Allen, Trevor Morgan, Paul Crompton, John Impey, Derek Dawkins, Harry Redknapp, coach, and David Webb, manager. Front row, Tony Funnell, Chris Sulley, Kevin Dawtry, Keith Williams, Steve Carter, Milton Graham and Brian O'Donnell. Wearing smart new tracksuits which they will take with them on a trip to New Zealand, by invitation from the New Zealand FA (below centre)

■ Kenny Allen, May 1981 (far right)

■ Captain John Impey receives Mecca Loyalty Award for 200 league appearances from Jo Lucy, general manager of Tiffany's (above)

The Cherries
1980-1983

In association with:

cmp
Print Solutions

■ George Best running onto the pitch and in action for AFC Bournemouth against Newport County in League Division 3 in March 1983 (here and left)

■ George Best made his Third Division debut for AFC Bournemouth against Newport County at Dean Court

■ Fans celebrate winning Division 3 title at Fulham (right)

■ Harry Redknapp. Bournemouth v Rotherham United 9th May 1987 (below)

■ Harry Redknapp and Jimmy Gabriel celebrate winning the Division 3 title (bottom centre)

■ Jubilant John Williams and Tony Pulis (far right)

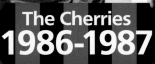

The Cherries
1986-1987

■ AFC Bournemouth win the Division 3 title at Fulham on 4th May 1987

■ John Williams celebrates (far left)

■ Tony Sealy and Harry Redknapp, AFCB v Rotherham United, 9th May 1987 (left)

■ Presenting the boardroom 'team' behind the team at Dean Court (below left)

■ Harry Redknapp holds aloft the Third Division Championship trophy (below)

■ Cherries celebrate their league title win at the home game against Rotherham at Dean Court on 9th May 1987

■ Cherries training (above)
■ Jamie Redknapp does a spot of painting at Dean Court (below)

■ Luther Blissett celebrates Cherries' 5th goal in their 5-4 victory over Hull City (left)
■ AFC Bournemouth v Oldham, 14th October 1989 (right)
■ Kevin Bond against Portsmouth (below right)
■ Bournemouth's Shaun Teale against Bradford City (below)

The Cherries
1989-1990

■ Leeds United fans riot at King's Park in May 1990

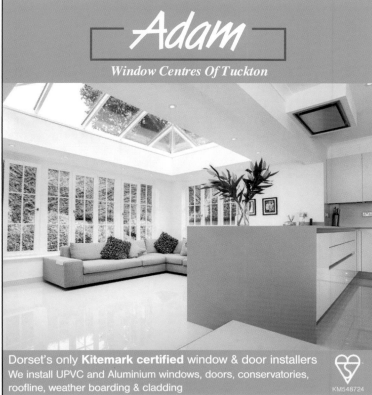

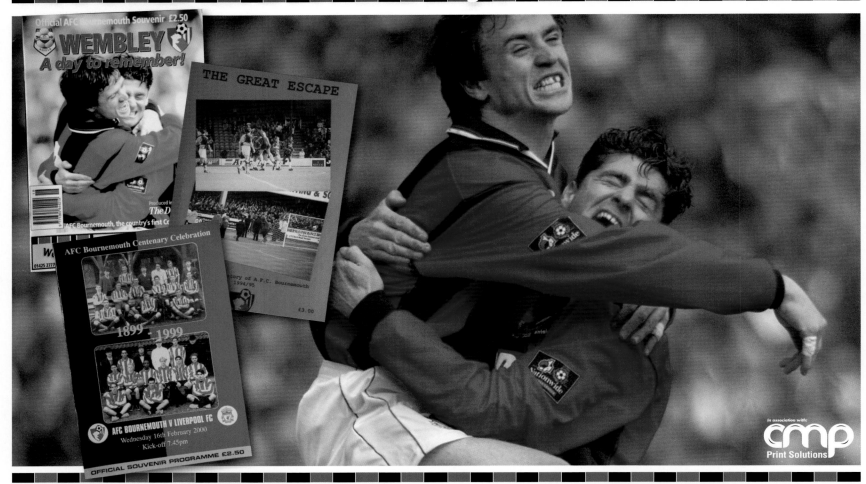

THE 1990s started with Bournemouth struggling to stay in the old Division Two – and everything came down to a bank holiday clash with Leeds United.

An estimated 6,000 Leeds fans came to Bournemouth that May weekend, many without tickets, and a hard core of them ran riot through the town.

On the pitch, Leeds' 1-0 victory ended Bournemouth's three years in the second division.

That summer, Harry Redknapp went to Italy for the World Cup with Brian Tiler, who had been the club's managing director. They were involved in road accident in which Tiler died, along with three young people in a sportscar that was on the wrong side of the road.

Redknapp left the club in 1992 and was succeeded by Tony Pulis. The club was suffering destabilising financial problems, the stadium was in poor repair and despite signings such as future legend Steve Fletcher, results were getting worse.

The 1994-95 season saw the Cherries struggling to avoid relegation from the new Division Two. Pulis was sacked, to be replaced by Mel Machin, and the team pulled off their 'Great Escape' from relegation.

But financial problems were worsening, and in 1997, the receivers were called in.

A meeting was held at the Winter Gardens concert hall, where £35,000 was donated in cash and a group of supporters announced a trust fund to buy the stadium.

The resulting stay of execution enabled the Cherries to make their first Wembley appearance in the final of the Auto Windscreens Shield in 1998.

They lost 2-1 to Grimsby after a "golden goal" in extra time; but being at Wembley at all seemed like a miracle.

In association with:
cmp Print Solutions

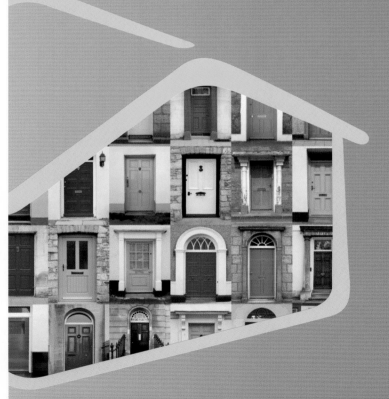

THE CHERRIES: 1890 to the Premier League

- AFC Bournemouth pre-season training 23rd June 1990 (left)
- Cherries players off to Army Camp. Young reserve keeper David McCarthy grabs probably his only opportunity ever to tell 6"1 Trevor Aylott, second left, what to do (bottom left)
- Efan Ekoku, left, and Luther Blissett (right)
- Paul Morrell, left, Harry Redknapp, centre, and Luther Blissett, right (below)
- Trevor Aylott AFC Bournemouth v Fulham 29th September 1990. 3-0 League Division Three (bottom right)

The Cherries 1990-1991

In association with: **cmp** Print Solutions

- AFC Bournemouth players get called up to Army Camp

The Cherries
1990-1991

In association with:

cmp
Print Solutions

■ Sean O'Driscoll's 300th league game for Bournemouth. Left to right Luther Blissett, Paul Morrell, Sean O'Driscoll and Andy Jones (above)

■ Andy Jones signing for AFC Bournemouth 25th Oct 1990 (below)

■ Jamie Redknapp in action for Bournemouth v Gillingham in the Leyland Daf Cup (right)

■ Short lived joy for Andy Jones and fans as the players mob Morrell. AFC lose the game 3-1 at Shrewsbury Town

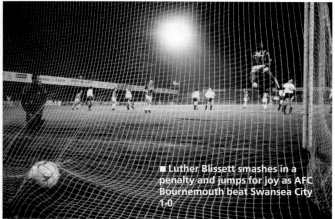

■ Luther Blissett smashes in a penalty and jumps for joy as AFC Bournemouth beat Swansea City 1-0

The Cherries 1991-1993
In association with: **cmp** Print Solutions

■ Harry Redknapp urges his players on against Newcastle United (above)

■ New signing Jimmy Case with manager Harry Redknapp, 3rd July 1991 (top left)

■ Fences come down at Dean Court 22nd June 1991 (left)

■ Denny Mundee scores Cherries' second goal as the Barnet keeper scrambles in vain (top right)

■ Denny Mundee ends up in the net as Bournemouth beat Cheltenham 3-0 (right)

■ Matt Holland with begging bowl asking people to donate money to save the club January 1997

**The Cherries
1996-1997**

CHERRIES: Nationwide Division Two

CRASH! – 85 minutes and five seconds
BANG! – 86 minutes and 44 seconds
WALLOP! – 87 minutes and 25 seconds

Wade Elliott set it back to Brian Stock who whipped a great ball in. I gambled at the near post and flicked it in
James Hayter on first goal

Gareth O'Connor played a great ball through and I just ran on to it and slotted between the keeper's legs
James Hayter on second goal

Warren Cummings slipped the ball to me, I took a touch and hit across the goal-keeper into the far corner.
James Hayter on third goal

OH BOY!

New dad Hayter hits fastest hat-trick in League history...

KEEPSAKE: Super sub James Hayter holds on to the match ball after his historic hat-trick heroics last night

You came, you saw, they conquered!

By Melanie Vass

WE'VE DONE IT! The superstars say it all as the Cherries lift the cup after a Welsh goalfest at the Millennium Stadium

Were you at the Millennium Stadium on Saturday? Check out our

Daily ECHO

CHERRIES: PROMOTION WINNERS
20-PAGE SUPPLEMENT INSIDE

YOUR LOCAL NEWSPAPER • GOT A STORY? CALL: 01202 554601

MONDAY, MAY 26, 2003 No.39,385 32p

FAN-TASTIC!

By Andy Martin

WE DID IT! Steve Fletcher and Carl Fletcher hug on emotion at the Millennium Stadium on Saturday, where Cherries beat Lincoln City 5-2

WE'RE GOING UP

• 20-page match supplement inside • We were there, were you? p6-7

AILY ECHO

bournemouthecho.co.uk 40p

2 FOR 1 OFFER!
OF TASTY MEAL DEALS INSIDE

Cherries pull off the great escape!

Six pages of special coverage as AFC Bournemouth avoid the drop amid ecstatic scenes at Dean Court

Celebrate after Cherries' 2-1 win over Grimsby on Saturday. The victory the drop and will be playing league football next season. See our six reaction and photos capturing the drama. Picture: Colin Messer

afcb

BACK OF THE NET
Cherries v Colchester United

SPORT

FANCY A FLUTTER? RACING IS ON PAGE 44

The picture that says it all
>> SEE PAGES 49, 50, 51, 52-53

33% OFF

THE TWO THOUSANDS

Sean O'Driscoll, who had served the club in various posts, was elevated to the position of manager at the start of the 2000-2001 season with Mel Machin taking on a director of football role.

O'Driscoll's first season at the helm will be remembered for a Division Two play-off near-miss, inspired by West Ham loan signing Jermain Defoe, who famously scored 10 goals in 10 games after starting the run on his debut at Stoke.

However, despite his goalscoring exploits, Cherries were pipped to a play-off place on the final day of the season following an epic 3-3 draw at Reading.

O'Driscoll was unable to save Cherries from relegation the following season but a place in the play-offs was secured just 12 months later and the team bounced back at the first attempt.

A memorable May day at the Millennium Stadium in Cardiff saw Cherries overcome Lincoln 5-2 with club legend Steve Fletcher opening the scoring.

James Hayter scored a record-breaking hat-trick in 140 seconds against Wrexham the following season and, despite financial uncertainty, O'Driscoll managed to steady the ship until he left for Doncaster in October 2006.

O'Driscoll's successor Kevin Bond was unable to stave off relegation to the bottom flight in 2007-2008 while the club's future had been cast in doubt after it was placed into administration midway through the campaign.

Eddie Howe's appointment on New Year's Eve 2008 marked the dawn of an exciting and successful new era which started with a Houdini-like escape from relegation and continued with promotion to League One in 2009-2010.

In association with:

cmp
Print Solutions

■ Steve Fletcher wins another header, at home to Nuneaton Borough in the FA Cup second round (left)
■ Wade Elliott tries to ride a Nuneaton challenge (right)
■ Through to the third round: Richard Hughes and Wade Elliott celebrate the FA Cup win over Nuneaton (below)

The Cherries
2000-2002

In association with:
cmp
Print Solutions

■ A new home: After a winning start, the season ends with the Cherries relegated to Division 3

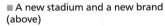

■ A new stadium and a new brand (above)
■ Carl Fletcher in action against Bristol Rovers (below)
■ November 2001 sees AFC Bournemouth beat Wrexham 3-0, in their first match at the new stadium (left)

THE CHERRIES: 1890 to the Premier League

■ Fans hoping for autographs in their testimonial programmes (left)

■ Mel acknowledges the support from the crowd as Juan Sebastian Veron and Ole Gunnar Solskjaer join in the applause (right)

■ Mel and Rio Ferdinand who also had a spell at Dean Court, on loan (bottom right)

The Cherries 2002-2003

In association with:
cmp Print Solutions

■ Thank you Mel: Manchester United come out with AFC Bournemouth for Mel Machin's testimonial match

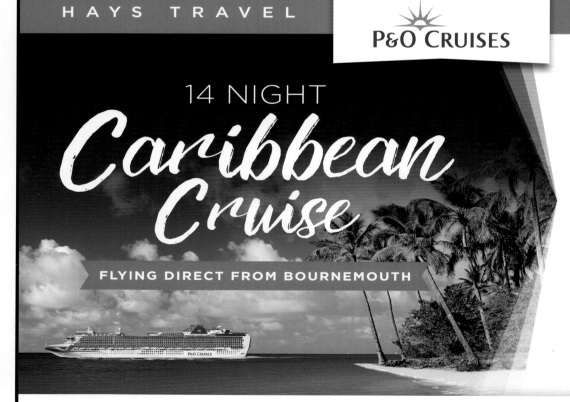

■ Cherries' first goal is appreciated by the lads looking over the fence (above) ■ Jason Tindall and colleagues get in and about Ryan Giggs, who takes it in good heart (below)

The Cherries
2002-2003

■ AFC Bournemouth celebrate promotion through the play-offs, and on the open-top bus parade

Nationwide
FOOTBALL LEAGUE
DIVISION 3 PLAY-OFF WINNERS 2003
A.F.C. BOURNEMOUTH

In association with:
cmp
Print Solutions

The Cherries
2014-2015

In association with:
cmp
Print Solutions

■ Dean Court in rapture. The unbelievable has come true! AFC Bournemouth have won promotion to the Premier League. Fans, players, manager and Chairman celebrate as one...

■ Monday 27th April 2015, Cherries v Bolton Wanderers, promotion to the Premier League is sealed

Unlock Bournemouth's Hidden World with an Augmented Reality Experience!

The 'Go Bournemouth Coast' app is giving you a chance to explore local businesses and experience Bournemouth's world-class coastal areas.

It's time to take part in a unique Bournemouth coastal experience, utilise the latest augmented reality technology and explore a fantastic array of local businesses! Funded by the Bournemouth Coastal BID, the 'Go Bournemouth Coast' app is providing a series of thrilling seasonally themed augmented reality character hunts and prize giveaways, so you can enjoy Bournemouth all through the year.

Suitable for people of all ages, you can simply download the app on your Android or iOS device and take part in fun and family-friendly activities. With over 100 participating businesses there's a wonderful abundance of shops, retailers, attractions and eateries to discover. Celebrate Easter, go

vintage for Shake n' Stir and get adventurous during the summer! Check out the app today for a full diary of events, as well as notifications about special VIP treats, prizes and virtual characters.

Participating businesses are located along the popular and beautiful coastal districts of Westbourne, West Cliff, Bournemouth Seafront, East Cliff, Boscombe, Southbourne, Pokesdown, Tuckton and Hengistbury Head.

To download the 'Go Bournemouth Coast' app and find out more information, visit: www.gobournemouthcoast.co.uk.

All content correct at time of print. Please check online for latest updates.. T&C's apply: Minimum age for app: 4+ years old. Minimum age for competition: 14+ years old

Bournemouth
COASTAL BID

Download the app & scan the logo to start!

 @bournemouthseasons   @bmthseasons

GO
Bournemouth
COAST

"IT'S ALL ABOUT TOMORROW AND WHAT YOU ACHIEVE NEXT..."

EDDIE Howe outlined his hopes for the calendar year after contemplating a rollercoaster 2017 in charge of Cherries.

Boss Howe guided his troops to a club-record ninth-place finish in the Premier League last season.

Cherries are currently 12th in the top flight but are among a clutch of sides aiming to distance themselves from the bottom three.

And Howe is hoping AFC Bournemouth "continues to grow on and off the pitch" over the next 12 months.

He told the Daily Echo: "Last year was a good year, although given the position we ended it in, it was sometimes very difficult to see that.

"But when you take things as a whole, we finished ninth in the Premier League. That's unprecedented for us and has to be a huge high.

"It was incredible to finish in the top half, something we would only have dreamed about a few years ago.

"The players deserve a lot of credit and, hopefully, those memories will serve them well for what they encounter for the rest of this season.

"We are going to be defined by what we do in the latter stages of this campaign.

"It's all about tomorrow and what you achieve next, it's not about what you have done historically.

"My hopes for this year are that the club continues to grow on and off the pitch. There always has to be an upward trajectory for the club, from top to bottom.

"We have still got a lot to do to reach the level of the other teams in the division we're competing in, with facilities being one example.

"Another wish is that we never lose sight of where we came from, our expectations and the challenges we face, and that we stay united.

"Our togetherness as a club has always been unique and it's very important we maintain and enhance that."

In association with:

cmp
Print Solutions

In association with:

cmp Print Solutions

EDDIE Howe insisted there should be no disappointment over Cherries' 12th-place finish in the Premier League and said: "These are unprecedented times."

Howe guided Cherries to their second-best finish in English football with victory at Burnley on Sunday, beaten only by the ninth-place effort of the previous campaign.

The Dorset outfit finished 16th in the 2015-16 Premier League season and have spent the rest of their history in the lower divisions.

Reflecting on the campaign, Howe told the Daily Echo: "I think it's a huge achievement. I think the problem we created was that finishing ninth was the mark last season and people are maybe disappointed with 12th.

"But I think it's more of a compliment to what we did last season than a criticism of what we did this season.

"You have to look at the teams who finished below us, the history of those clubs and the size of the clubs who have been relegated compared to ours.

"It was a huge effort from the players. Of course, we always want to do better

and even when we finished ninth last season, I wanted to do better than that.

"That will never leave me so I know there are things we can work on and a lot of things we can analyse and do better but, ultimately, you have to say it's a great job by the players."

Cherries' ability to mix it with the best in the top flight following a rapid rise through the Football League resulted in raised expectations among supporters.

Put to him that it would be easy to forget it had been Cherries' second-best season, Howe said:
"It's easy to forget a lot of things.

"It's easy to get wrapped up in the day-to-day thing of what we're doing in the Premier League.

"But this club has only been in the Premier League for three seasons in its history and these are unprecedented times.

"We have to, in my opinion, give the players all the encouragement and

support we can because they have never let this club down.

"Hopefully, the supporters have enjoyed this incredible journey we have been on and, hopefully, it's not over yet and we have a lot more success to enjoy."

Joshua King and Callum Wilson finished as Cherries' joint top scorers in the Premier League having netted eight goals apiece, their nearest rivals being Ryan Fraser and Junior Stanislas, who both got five.

Winger Jordon Ibe was the leading assist-maker on six with Andrew Surman second on five, while Simon Francis topped the standings for most completed passes.

The captain made 1,606 in total, finishing ahead of fellow defenders Nathan Ake (1,589) and Charlie Daniels (1,568).

Francis was the only Cherries man to be sent off in the league this season having been dismissed for two bookable offences in the 4-0 win over Huddersfield Town in November.

In association with:

EDDIE Howe insisted there should be no disappointment over Cherries' 12th-place finish in the Premier League and said: "These are unprecedented times."

Howe guided Cherries to their second-best finish in English football with victory at Burnley on Sunday, beaten only by the ninth-place effort of the previous campaign.

The Dorset outfit finished 16th in the 2015-16 Premier League season and have spent the rest of their history in the lower divisions.

Reflecting on the campaign, Howe told the Daily Echo: "I think it's a huge achievement. I think the problem we created was that finishing ninth was the mark last season and people are maybe disappointed with 12th.

"But I think it's more of a compliment to what we did last season than a criticism of what we did this season.

"You have to look at the teams who finished below us, the history of those clubs and the size of the clubs who have been relegated compared to ours.

"It was a huge effort from the players. Of course, we always want to do better and even when we finished ninth last season, I wanted to do better than that.

"That will never leave me so I know there are things we can work on and a lot of things we can analyse and do better but, ultimately, you have to say it's a great job by the players."

Cherries' ability to mix it with the best in the top flight following a rapid rise through the Football League resulted in raised expectations among supporters.

Put to him that it would be easy to forget it had been Cherries' second-best season, Howe said: "It's easy to forget a lot of things.

"It's easy to get wrapped up in the day-to-day thing of what we're doing in the Premier League.

"But this club has only been in the Premier League for three seasons in its history and these are unprecedented times.

"We have to, in my opinion, give the players all the encouragement and support we can because they have never let this club down.

"Hopefully, the supporters have enjoyed this incredible journey we have been on and, hopefully, it's not over yet and we have a lot more success to enjoy."

Joshua King and Callum Wilson finished as Cherries' joint top scorers in the Premier League having netted eight goals apiece, their nearest rivals being Ryan Fraser and Junior Stanislas, who both got five.

Winger Jordon Ibe was the leading assist-maker on six with Andrew Surman second on five, while Simon Francis topped the standings for most completed passes.

The captain made 1,606 in total, finishing ahead of fellow defenders Nathan Ake (1,589) and Charlie Daniels (1,568).

Francis was the only Cherries man to be sent off in the league this season having been dismissed for two bookable offences in the 4-0 win over Huddersfield Town in November.

In association with:
cmp
Print Solutions

Cherries Boss Eddie Howe said some "really big points" on the road had been pivotal in helping Cherries guarantee a fourth successive season in the Premier League.

Second-half goals from Joshua King and Callum Wilson saw Cherries bring down the curtain on their campaign with a dramatic 2-1 win at Burnley.

A fourth victory on their travels secured 12th place for Howe's men and earned the club around £18million in prize money.

Cherries, who also won at Stoke, Newcastle and Chelsea, bettered by three last season's away points total.

They registered 22 in their first season in the top flight.

Asked specifically about the away record, Howe told the Daily Echo: "We didn't have the number of wins we would have liked but we were competitive.

"We picked up a number of draws that, when you look back, were really big points for us and massive moments when we didn't lose games we could have.

"The points at Crystal Palace and Leicester were huge, even if we were frustrated we didn't hold on against Leicester.

That was a really important point.

"We showed a really good mentality away from home but without maybe the dominating performances that we would have associated ourselves with at times in previous seasons."

EDDIE Howe has tipped striker Joshua King to rediscover his goalscoring best for Cherries next season.

King netted his eighth Premier League goal to spark Cherries' comeback during their 2-1 win over Burnley on the final day of the season.

It was his sixth goal in his past 13 games, having racked up 16 in the previous campaign.

Howe believes King has perhaps fallen prey to the second-season syndrome of opponents looking to stifle him at every turn.

But he still backed the Norway forward to come good in the long run: "Josh hasn't hit the heights of last season where he was absolutely outstanding.

"One of the big reasons for us finishing as high as we did and doing as well as we did was having a striker who scored 16 goals.

"The second season after a season like that, it's difficult to replicate, it's difficult to do it again.

"I think he's had a good season, he's played his part, been versatile and shown a good attitude.

"He will feel he wants more goals, but he's definitely contributed to the team and that's hugely important, without him maybe hitting the highs of last season.

"Consistency is difficult. Teams went into this season knowing more about him and possibly coming with game plans to try to stop him, knowing he was one of our main threats. Having to work a way around that is difficult.

"But he has performed well for the team, you can't underestimate that. He's been a big part of another season of success for us.

"I back him to go again next season and think he can have another big season for us."

BOSS Eddie Howe hopes Cherries can ward off interest in prized assets Nathan Ake and Lewis Cook so he can continue to "build a team around them".

Ake and Cook have both enjoyed outstanding individual campaigns, playing starring roles in helping Cherries secure a fourth successive season in the Premier League.

Defender Ake, Cherries' club record £20million signing from Chelsea, swept the board by winning all the club's player-of-the-year awards in his first season at Vitality Stadium.

And midfielder Cook, a £7m buy from Leeds two years ago, capped his exploits for Cherries by forcing his way into the reckoning for England's World Cup squad.

With Howe predicting a "big transfer window" for Cherries, he knows keeping the likes of Ake and Cook will be key for the club's future.

Asked whether he had any concerns about losing either player, Howe replied: "If it happens, it happens and there is nothing I can do about it.

"Both players have had outstanding seasons and our wish would be to keep them, build the team around them and not sell them.

"You want players performing well at Premier League level because, ultimately, that is how you are going to win games.

"If they do that consistently then naturally they will be linked with other clubs. That is part of the process and we have always had that here."

Howe said he and his staff were looking to unearth the next Ake or Cook with the club's recruitment policy continuing to focus on promising young players.

Discussing his plans for the summer, Howe said: "We are going to need to do certain things and are going to need to be active in the market.

"We have seen the emergence of some really important young players this season. It is very important the team continues to evolve and we can't stand still.

"We are never going to be able to sign established Premier League players who are in their prime. It is just not going to happen and we are well aware of that so have to choose a route to go down in terms of our recruitment.

"More often than not, we have tried to sign young players and develop and improve them so when they are in their prime, they can step into the Premier League.

"It won't always work and you will get one or two wrong along the way. In the main, that is probably still the healthiest way for us to recruit because you get the long-term benefits when they are established.

"Ryan Fraser would be a really good example of how we look to recruit. He took a long time to get into the team, as we knew he would when we signed him.

"But he is now an established Premier League player. Hopefully, we will get the benefit long term of his recent success.

"How you identify those players is the tricky bit."

Farmer Palmers is

Celebrating **20** years

of family entertainment, an awesome team and the dedication of a selfless family

The secret is out, and children are shouting about it! The "must visit" Dorset destination for families who's priority is giving their children fantastic fun is Farmer Palmer's! If you are looking for the worst kept secret in Dorset, and you have children aged 8 years and under, there is only one place to head for! What makes them so special? Teamwork. The attraction is family run so they totally understand the needs of families with young children.

Amazingly they have been marking milestones and making family memories for 20 years!

Look around the Farm Park. You can see grandparents sharing their life skills with excited grandchildren. Parents leaving their chores, and devices behind to stretch their imaginations with their 'Mini Me's' and of course the all the little VIPS. The antics of the children having fun, making friends and learning is simply priceless.

The most remarkable endorsement is the formation of a side that consists of engaging, helpful and polite teenagers

proves that grassroots is where it is at!

The Farmer Palmers Customer Experience Life Cycle starts with the Children, babies, toddlers and primary school superstars visiting over and over and becoming part of our Farmer Palmer Family (often with annual passes)!

From 13 years they can apply for their first job. Sadly we can not employ everyone who wants to work here but we are so lucky to work with awesome young people who have a desire to help!

Work Experience? Farmer Palmer's has supported many students in their first taste of work.

The experienced team is totally committed to giving 110 % to the whole Farmer Palmer's experience with current and previous employees now visiting with children and Annual Passes of their own. Making us their children's 2nd home!

Have you met Farmer Palmer's chef Dylan? He worked for Phillip and Sandra Palmer when he was a teenager.

Now a dad himself, he has gone full circle and is making fab meals for the children of Dorset and beyond!

Together we have successfully made Farmer Palmer's a household name in Dorset and fare firmly fixed into the memories of families and children who grow up here.

They are looking at the next 20 years, so, by our sums – this means that the children who visited the park when it opened back in 1998 will be bringing their own children to the park – now that's how to keep your customer numbers up!

"All the dedicated staff have an excellent attitude. They're friendly, approachable and as we have found again and again over the years, totally understanding of the needs of parents with little ones. They are kind, keen to offer help, smile and all because they love what they do, and totally committed to giving 110 % to the whole Farmer Palmer's experience. The attention to 'safe fun' is more than reassuring"

Farmer Palmers supports grass roots football clubs

Farmer Palmers has been supporting local Under 8's grassroots football teams for many years. Seeing the children's happy faces and hearing the feedback as they grow and develop is a personal reward that warms the heart.

Coaches, we congratulate you for your motivation and patience! Linesmen we praise you for your dedication! We totally recognise the hard work and commitment of the coaches and adults who give up hours a week to help children in all areas of sport. We honour their teamwork, leadership and a genuine passion for what they do! To aim for success the team talk, training, training and more training is what going for goal and awards is all about. Watching the children's faces and banter when their effort is rewarded with the Cup, is a memory never forgotten.

We've all done it. Standing on the edge of a football pitch in the middle of an icy winter. Being an over enthusiastic parent shouting "encouragement" from the side lines not realising all we were doing was confusing the children and not respecting the referee! It can be frustrating watching 5 children chase the same ball and feeling you could do a better job.

Suddenly the moment comes when you are elated and feeling immensely proud when your son/daughter as they make THE pass that secures the ball to the striker or scores that all important goal!

Farmer Palmer's original ethos of keeping the experience of our Customers a personal one is also reflected in the way they are proud to give back to the community. It is something special that they do not really shout about.

"Can I start by wholeheartedly thanking you for sponsoring the boys for their jackets and for your logo to be added to our match day shirts this season, they have been so proud that Farmer Palmers are their sponsors. Many of the opposing teams have commented on how lucky we are to have you as their sponsors. All the adults involved in the team, myself, my coaches and the parents would all also like to convey our appreciation to you also as the confidence it gave the boys was immense.

The boys have all progressed beyond my wildest dreams this season and they all continue to love their football which is my main aim. The group of players continues to grow and I currently have 15 kids (boys and girls) training with me on a Friday night which is fantastic for the club and the team.

Please see below a picture of the new team in their new match day kits and jumpers. Thank you so, so much your continued support gives them all so much pleasure and means so much to them and us"

Greg Partridge

Dexter Sports YFC 2 years U8's Lions: & U8's Leopards Match day kits, Jackets, GK Kit

"Having sponsorship for the team means that all the children can dress the same and this helps them feel like more of a team. The best bit for me about coaching other than seeing the children enjoy themselves is watching them learn and improve and how proud they are when the practice pays off and watching them grow as individuals and even more so as a team. Coach at Lytchett Red Triangle, Lytchett Matravers"

Football Kits for the players at Lytchett and Upton Red Triangle U8's Tornadoes with Kevin Watson.

We have supported countless charities and organisation in 2017, including: Greenfields YFC, Portcastrian football Club, Harlequin & Weston Sports, Cadets, Blandford United FC, Becky Heeks Cup for Football, etc, Cheerleeders Education, Fundraising events, golf, sports Guides, PTA , Rugby Clubs, Young Achievers, Youth Scouts.